zen doodle journaling

Creative Reflections

Color & Write for Mindfulness

Illustrations by
Nikolett Corley

ST. MARTIN'S GRIFFIN
NEW YORK

How to Use
Your Coloring Journal

Let this therapeutic journal be a source of inspiration and relaxation whenever you need it. Simply open the journal to your favorite illustration and color your way to a peaceful and reflective state of mind. Consider the accompanying journal question as you personalize each design with a rainbow of color. Let your thoughts wander until you feel moved to express them in writing. Feel free to use this artistic journal whenever you need a creative escape or a mindful moment.

This Journal Belongs to:

_____

What difficulty
has made you stronger?

What seems to us as bitter trials are often blessings in disguise.
—OSCAR WILDE

Describe something
spontaneous you have done.

Follow your inner moonlight; don't hide the madness.

—ALLAN GINSBERG

What would you like to spend more time doing?

We become what we think about most of the time, and that's the strangest secret.

—EARL NIGHTINGALE

What is your
definition of success?

An artist cannot fail. It is a success just to be one.

–Charles Horton Cooley

Whom have you loved with all your heart?

... and, in her starry shade
Of dim and solitary loveliness,
I learn'd the language of another world.
—LORD BYRON

What fears
do you hope to overcome?

To live a creative life, we must lose our fear of being wrong.
—JOSEPH CHILTON PEARCE

For what
are you thankful?

_____

_____

_____

_____

_____

_____

_____

_____

_____

_____

_____

_____

_____

_____

_____

_____

_____

When you rise in the morning,
give thanks for the light, for your life, for your strength.

—TECUMSEH

What inner quality makes you beautiful?

As we grow old, the beauty steals inward.

—RALPH WALDO EMERSON

Where would you like to travel?

Though we travel the world over to find the beautiful,
we must carry it with us, or we find it not.
—RALPH WALDO EMERSON

What Turns a bad day into a good one?

Just when the caterpillar thought the world was ending, he turned into a butterfly.

—PROVERB

What makes you unique?

Try not to become a man of success,
but rather try to become a man of value.
–ALBERT EINSTEIN

What fascinates you
about the world?

_I believe the world is incomprehensibly beautiful —
an endless prospect of magic and wonder._

—ANSEL ADAMS

What are you searching for?

When you stop chasing the wrong things,
you give the right things a chance to catch you.

—LOLLY DASKAL

What sights or sounds relax you?

Let things flow naturally forward in whatever way they like.

−*Lao Tzu*

From what doubts and worries are you ready to free yourself?

It is not the mountain we conquer, but ourselves.
—EDMUND HILLARY

What goals do you have in sight?

I know of no more encouraging fact than
the unquestionable ability of man to elevate
his life by conscious endeavor.
—HENRY DAVID THOREAU

What beautiful thing
did you notice Today?

Anyone who keeps the ability to see beauty never grows old.
−FRANZ KAFKA

What choices have influenced your path in life?

May your trails be crooked, winding, lonesome,
dangerous, leading to the most amazing view.

—EDWARD ABBEY

How well do you treat yourself?

_You yourself, as much as anybody in the entire universe,
deserve your love and affection._

–Unknown

What is one of your favorite childhood memories?

A multitude of small delights constitute happiness.

–CHARLES BAUDELAIRE

With whom do you
share your deepest feelings?

Drawing is feeling. Color is an act of reason.
—PIERRE BONNARD

Who or what never fails to make you laugh?

Earth laughs in flowers.

—RALPH WALDO EMERSON

What activity gives you a sense of peace?

The greatest gift of a garden is the restoration of the five senses.

—HANNA RION

What color describes your mood today?

Colors speak all languages.

—JOSEPH ADDISON

What makes you feel hopeful?

I find hope in the darkest of days, and focus in the brightest.

—DALAI LAMA

What prediction can you make about your future?

_____

_____

_____

_____

_____

_____

_____

_____

_____

_____

_____

_____

_____

_____

_____

_____

_____

_____

_____

The world is your kaleidoscope.
–JAMES ALLEN

When have you surprised yourself?

In the middle of winter, I at last discovered
that there was in me an invincible summer.
–ALBERT CAMUS

If you could live anywhere, where would you live?

It is good to know our universe. What is new is only new to us.

–PEARL S. BUCK

Where do you feel like you belong?

I am a part of all that I have met.

—ALFRED LORD TENNYSON

What tests your patience?

Adopt the pace of Nature. Her secret is patience.

—RALPH WALDO EMERSON

Describe a perfect day.

Every day is a journey, and the journey itself is home.
–MATSUO BASHO

What have you discovered about the world?

We live only to discover beauty. All else is a form of waiting.

–KAHLIL GIBRAN

What time of year suits you best?

In seed time learn, in harvest teach, in winter enjoy.
—WILLIAM BLAKE

Where do you gather inspiration?

One sees great things from the valley;
only small things from the peak.
–G. K. CHESTERTON

What have you
learned about yourself?

There are some things you learn best in calm, and some in storm.

—WILLA CATHER

What brings you joy?

A thing of beauty is a joy for ever:
Its loveliness increases; it will never
Pass into nothingness.
—JOHN KEATS

What do you wish to know?

Believe those who seek the truth, doubt those who find it.
—ANDRÉ GIDE

What adds excitement and color to your life?

Color is the fruit of life.

—GUILLAUME APOLLINAIRE

Describe a time when you tried something new.

Colors are brighter when the mind is open.

—ADRIANA ALARCON

When do you feel
most connected to nature?

In all things of nature there is something of the marvelous.

−ARISTOTLE

What change are you looking forward to?

Autumn is a second spring when every leaf is a flower.

—ALBERT CAMUS

How has life been kind to you?

I am rich today with autumn's gold.

—GLADYS HARP

What adventure awaits you?

We must go and see for ourselves.
—JACQUES COUSTEAU

What makes you a better person?

Today I have grown taller from walking with the trees.

–KARLE WILSON BAKER

What is the best way to end a day?

I have loved the stars too fondly to be fearful of the night.

—SARAH WILLIAMS

In what do you have faith?

Keep your faith in all beautiful things.
In the sun when it is hidden.
In the spring when it is gone.
—ROY ROLFE GILSON

What do you wish would never change?

Nothing endures but change.

—HERACLITUS

What were the
highlights of your day?

How we spend our days is, of course,
how we spend our lives.
—Annie Dillard

When do you crave solitude?

Do not feel lonely, the entire universe is inside you.

–RUMI

Describe one of
your happiest moments.

Happiness is a butterfly, which when pursued,
is always beyond your grasp, but which,
if you will sit down quietly, may alight upon you.

—UNKNOWN

Whom do you want to become?

Life is not about finding yourself.
Life is about creating yourself.
—GEORGE BERNARD SHAW

Write down
Ten positive Thoughts.

It's not what you look at that matters, it's what you see.
−HENRY DAVID THOREAU

How would you enjoy starting each day?

You've got to get up every morning with determination if you're going to go to bed with satisfaction.

—GEORGE LORIMER

What three things

do you desire most?

In my experience, there is only one motivation, and that is desire.
No reasons or principle contain it or stand against it.

–JANE SMILEY

When have you taken a chance on something?

It is better to fail in originality, than to succeed in imitation.

—HERMAN MELVILLE

What is the most generous thing someone has done for you?

Beauty is not in the face; beauty is a light in the heart.
−KAHLIL GIBRAN

How could you add more fun to your life?

People rarely succeed unless they have fun in what they are doing.

—DALE CARNEGIE

What expectations do you have for the coming year?

*There are far, far better things ahead
than any we leave behind.*

–C.S. LEWIS

What do you value most in life?

Your life is not a problem to be
solved but a gift to be opened.

−Wayne Muller

How would you describe yourself?

No need to hurry. No need to sparkle.
No need to be anybody but oneself.

—VIRGINIA WOOLF

What captivates you
about the natural world?

If you truly love Nature, you will find beauty everywhere.
–Van Gogh

What do you like most about art?

Art washes away from the soul the dust of everyday life.

–PABLO PICASSO